TBRILLIANT
THOUGHTS

QAND PROVACATIVE
QUESTIONS

BRILLIANT THOUGHTS AND PROVACATIVE QUESTIONS

PAUL KARASIK

JOY OF LIVING PUBLISHING

Published by: Joy of Living Publishing, 952 Manhattan Beach Blvd., Ste. 200, Manhattan Beach, CA 90266

To order *Brilliant Thoughts and Provocative Questions* by mail, include $20.00 plus $3.00 for shipping and handling, or call 310-545-4994.

Joy of Living books are available at special quantity discounts for bulk purchases for fundraising, premiums and educational needs. Special editions or book excerpts can also be created for your specific needs. Call for pricing and details.

Website: www.paulkarasik.com

Publisher's Catalogue-in-Publishing
(Provided by Quality Books, Inc.)

Karasik, Paul, 1947-
    Brilliant thought and provocative questions /
    Paul Karasik. -- 1st ed.
       p. cm -- (Brilliant thoughts series)
       LCCN: 99-98242
       ISBN: 978-1-4675-8596-5

    1. Quotations, English. 2. Inspiration--
    Quotations, maxims, etc. 3. Self-actualization
    (Psychology) 4. Self-help techniques--Quotations,
    maxims, etc. I. Title.

PN6081.K37 2000   082
                        QBI00-900294

Cover Design: Frank Lacey
Layout and Typesetting: Pamela Terry
Editing: Virginia Iorio

Printed in the United States of America

10 9 8 7 6 5 4 3 2 1

ACKNOWLEDGMENTS

My sincere thanks and deepest respect to the great thinkers of the world. Your brilliant thoughts shed eternal light on the art and joy of living.

What is the hardest task in the world?
To think.

Ralph Waldo Emerson

CONTENTS

INTRODUCTION

It's easy to get lost. It's so easy to lose sight of what is important and what are merely details.

It has been my experience that when I fill my mind with noble thoughts, I feel better. I am more capable of discernment. It's then much easier to make choices that fill my life with the people, activities and things that make my life more complete and satisfying.

This book is a collection of dynamic thoughts that can be guideposts for making wise decisions in your life. Not every quote will hit home for you. That's okay. Take what you need and leave the rest. Better yet, when you find a quote that is particularly meaningful to you, don't just say to yourself, "That's so true." Write it down and place it where you can see it every day. Savor the words. Use it as a springboard for deeper contemplation.

Accompanying these brilliant thoughts are questions that are important to ask yourself. These questions will help you integrate the thoughts, ideas and concepts into your life. Many of these questions will be difficult for you to answer.

Some are somewhat rhetorical. Others may provoke negative responses in you. The questions that you might find somewhat disconcerting are usually the ones that are most valuable because they reflect some part of yourself that needs to be examined more closely.

Take some time with this book. Relax with it. Share the thoughts and questions that are most meaningful to you with significant people in your life.

This book is meant to be a tool for remembering what is really important in your life and letting go of what are merely details.

LOVE

For one human being to love another human being:
that is perhaps the most difficult task
that has been entrusted to us,
the ultimate task,
the final test and proof,
the work for which
all other work is merely preparation.

Rainer Maria Rilke

To love at all is to be vulnerable.
Love anything, and your heart will certainly be wrung
and possibly broken.
If you want to make sure of keeping it intact,
you must give your heart to no one,
not even an animal.
Wrap it carefully round with hobbies and little luxuries;
avoid all entanglements;
lock it up safe in the casket or coffin of your selfishness.
But in that casket—safe, dark, motionless,
airless—it will change.
It will not be broken;
it will become unbreakable, impenetrable, irredeemable.
The only alternative to tragedy,
or at least the risk of tragedy, is damnation.
The only place outside of Heaven
where you can be perfectly safe
from the dangers and perturbations of love is Hell.

C.S. Lewis

 WHAT DOES THE EXPRESSION
"PERFECT RELATIONSHIP" MEAN TO YOU?

Some day,
after we have mastered the winds,
the waves, the tides, and gravity
we shall harness the energies of love.
Then for the second time
in the history of the world,
man will have discovered fire.

Pierre Teilhard de Chardin

 WOULD YOU ACCEPT $1,000,000 TO NEVER
AGAIN SEE SOMEONE YOU TRULY LOVE?

I believe that the reason of life
is for each of us simply to grow in love.
I believe that this growth in love will contribute
more than any other force
to establish the Kingdom of God on earth.

Leo Tolstoy

One word frees us of all the weight and pain of life:
That word is love.

Sophocles

The confrontation with death—
and the reprieve from it—
makes everything look so precious, so sacred,
so beautiful that I feel more strongly than ever
the impulse to love it, to embrace it,
and to let myself be overwhelmed by it.
My river has never looked so beautiful…
Death, and its ever present possibility,
makes love, passionate love, more possible.
I wonder if we could love passionately,
if ecstacy would be possible at all,
if we knew we'd never die.

Abraham Maslow

 IF TO TRULY LOVE SOMEONE MEANS
YOU WOULD DIE FOR THIS PERSON,
WHO DO YOU TRULY LOVE?

There is no religion without love, and people may
talk as much as they like about religion,
but if it does not teach them to be good and kind
to man and beast, it is all a sham.

Anna Sewell

13

Love is an extraordinary thing; without it, life is barren.
You may have many possessions
and sit in the seat of power,
but without the beauty and greatness of love,
life soon becomes misery and confusion.
Life implies... that those who are loved be wholly free
to grow in their fullness,
to be something greater than mere social machines.
Love does not compel,
either openly or through subtle threat
of duties and responsibilities.
When there's any form of compulsion
or exertion of authority there's no love.

J. Krishnamurti

 COULD YOU LOVE SOMEONE WHO **ALWAYS**
AGREED WITH YOU?

There is no difficulty that enough love will not conquer;
no disease that enough love will not heal;
no door that enough love will not open.

Emmet Fox

IF YOU COULD SEE LOVE IN
WOULD EVERYONE SEE LOVE

When the time comes that you feel love for someone,
be gentle.
Love has a delicate nature.
Never be rough with it or it will be completely destroyed.
Always distinguish the difference between love and desire.
Love gives pleasure; desire creates pressure.
Desire, loneliness, tension, and disappointment
can all deteriorate the delicate nature of true love.
To love is to be gentle.
Tender love is truly beneficial in any circumstance.
If love is not given gently, it becomes stormy.
Stormy love, like stormy weather, can never last long.

Hua-Ching Ni

In our life there is a single color,
as on the artist's palette,
which provides the meaning of life and art.
It is the color of love.

Marc Chagall

Great love—
The kind that illumines and transforms us—
always includes a keen awareness of limitation as well.
Though love may inspire us to expand
and develop in new ways,
we can never be all things to the one we love,
or someone other than who we are.
Yet once accepted,
limitation also helps us develop essential qualities,
such as patience, determination,
compassion, and humor.
When love comes down to earth—
bringing to light those dark corners
we would prefer to ignore,
encompassing all the different parts of who we are—
it gains depth and power.

John Welwood

You live that you may learn to love,
you love that you may learn to live.
No other lesson is required of you.

Mirdad

To love is the most important thing in life.
But what do we mean by love?
When you love someone because that person
loves you in return, surely that is not love.
To love is to have that extraordinary
feeling of affection without asking anything in return.

Krishnamurti

We are born of love.
It is the principle of existence,
and its only end.

Benjamin Disraeli

You will find as you look back upon your life
that the moments
when you have truly lived
are the moments
when you have done things in a spirit of love.

Henry Drummond

 HOW MANY THINGS DID YOU DO TODAY
IN A SPIRIT OF LOVE?

17

Love is that condition in which
the happiness of another person
is essential to your own.

Robert A. Heinlein

Oh, the comfort—the inexpressible comfort of
feeling safe with a person—
having neither to weigh thoughts or measure words,
but pouring them all right out, just as they are,
chaff and grain together;
certain that a faithful hand will take and sift them,
keep what is worth keeping,
and then with the breath of kindness blow the rest away.

Dinah Maria Mulock Craik

 WHO DESERVES YOUR LOVE THE MOST?

This is the true measure of love:
when we believe that we alone can love,
that no one could ever have loved so before us,
and that no one will ever love in the same way after us.

Johann von Goethe

Neither a lofty degree of intelligence
nor imagination nor both together
go to the making of genius.
Love, love, love,
that is the soul of genius.

Wolfgang Amadeus Mozart

To cheat oneself out of love
is the most terrible deception;
it is an eternal loss for which there is no reparation,
either in time or eternity.

Søren Kierkegaard

 WITHOUT LOVE, CAN YOU EVER KNOW
WHO YOU REALLY ARE?

When souls really touch,
it is forever.
Then place and time disappear,
and all that remains is the consciousness
that we are not alone in life.

Joan Chittister

Put away the book,
the description, the tradition, the authority,
and take the journey of self-discovery.
Love,
and don't be caught in opinions and ideas
about what love is or should be.
When you love,
everything will become right.
Love has its own action.
Love,
and you will know the blessings of it.
Keep away from the authority who tells you
what love is and what love is not.
No authority knows
and he who knows cannot tell.
Love,
and there is understanding.

J. Krishnamurti

Love—
stronger than death and harder than hell.

Meister Eckhart

PASSION

The course of human history is determined,
not by what happens in the skies,
but what takes place in our hearts.

Sir Arthur Keith

The only lasting beauty is the beauty of the heart.

Rumi

If you love what you do,
you will never work another day in your life.

Confucius

 ARE YOU DOING WHAT YOU LOVE?
AND IF NOT NOW, WHEN?

Often people attempt to live their lives backwards:
they try to have more things,
or more money
in order to do more of what they want
so that they will appear happier.
The way it actually works
is the reverse.
You must first be who you really are,
then,
do what you need to do,
in order to have what you want.

Margaret Young

If it falls your lot to be a street sweeper,
sweep streets as Michelangelo carved marble,
sweep streets as Beethoven composed music,
or Shakespeare wrote poetry.

Martin Luther King, Jr.

 HAVE YOU EVER STOPPED TO THINK, THE
PASSION YOU FEEL IS THE SAME PASSION
SHAKESPEARE AND BEETHOVEN AND
MICHELANGELO FELT?

Put your heart, mind, intellect, and soul
even to your smallest acts.
This is the secret of success.

Swami Sivananda

Good work is never done in cold blood:
heat is needed to forge anything.
Every great achievement is the story of a flaming heart.

A.C. Carlson

The man who can't dance thinks the band is no good.

Polish proverb

23

People say what we are seeking is a meaning for life …
I think what we are really seeking
is an experience of being alive,
so that the experiences on the purely physical plane
will have resonance within our innermost being and reality,
so that we actually feel the rapture of being alive.

Joseph Campbell

We don't remember days, we remember moments.

Cesare Pavese

 HOW SHOULD YOU LIVE RIGHT NOW,
KNOWING YOU WILL DIE?

The best and most beautiful
things in the world cannot be seen
or even touched.
They must be felt with the heart.

Helen Keller

The heart has its reasons that the mind knows nothing of.

Blaise Pascal

Many men die at twenty-five and
aren't buried until they are seventy-five.

Benjamin Franklin

 WHAT CAN YOU DO TO FAN THE FLAME
THAT BURNS IN YOUR HEART?

Live—decently, fearlessly, joyously—
and don't forget that in the long run
it is not the years in your life
but the life in your years that counts!

Adlai Stevenson

Ask what the world needs.
Ask yourself what makes you come alive.
And then go out and do that.
Because what the world needs is
people who have come alive.

Harold Thurman Whitman

Passion is like genius: a miracle.

Romain Rolland

It is only with the heart that one can see rightly.
What is essential is invisible to the eye.

Antoine de Saint-Exupéry

I have often thought the best way
to define a man's character
would be to seek out the particular
mental or moral attitude in which,
when it came upon him,
he felt himself most deeply and intensely
active and alive.
At such moments there is a voice inside
which speaks and says:
"This is the real me!"

William James

 WHAT ARE YOU DOING WHEN YOU SAY
TO YOURSELF, "THIS IS THE REAL ME"?

Let yourself be silently drawn
by the stronger pull of what you really love.

Rumi

When people's dogs and chicks are lost
they go out and look for them
and yet the people who have lost their hearts
do not go out and look for them.
The principle of self-cultivation consists
in nothing but
trying to look for the lost heart.

Mencius

 CAN YOU DANCE LIKE THERE IS
NO ONE WATCHING?
CAN YOU LOVE LIKE YOU'LL
NEVER GET HURT?

You don't get to choose how you're going to die.
Or when.
You can only decide how you're going to live.
Now.

Joan Baez

You can't change the music of your soul.

Katharine Hepburn

To believe your own thought,
to believe that what is true for you in your own heart
is true for all men—that is genius.
A man should learn to detect and watch the gleam
of light which flashes across his mind from within,
more than the luster of the firmament of bards and sages.
Yet he dismisses without notice his thought,
because it is his thought, because it is his.
In every work of genius
we recognize our own rejected thoughts;
they come back to us with a certain alienated majesty.

Ralph Waldo Emerson

 CAN YOU STAY TRUE TO YOUR HEART
WHEN CHOOSING YOUR PATH?

It seems to me we can never give up
longing and wishing while we are thoroughly alive.
There are certain things we feel to be
beautiful and good,
and we must hunger after them.

George Eliot

28

...And O that awful deepdown torrent O and the sea
the sea crimson sometimes like fire and the glorious
sunsets and the figtrees in the Alemeda gardens yes
and all the queer little streets and pink
and blue and yellow houses and
the rosegardens and the jessamine
and geraniums and cactuses and Gilbraltar
as a girl where I was a Flower of the mountains yes when I
put the rose in my hair like the Andalusian girls used
or shall I wear a red yes and
how he kissed me under the Moorish wall and
I thought well
as well him as another and
then I asked him with my eyes to ask again
yes and then he asked me would I yes to say yes
my mountain flower and first I put my arms around him
yes and drew him down to me
so he could feel my breasts all perfume
yes and his heart was going like mad
and yes I said yes
I will Yes.

                                        James Joyce

MANIFESTING YOUR POWER

Growth and change take place
when a person has risked himself
and dares to become involved with
experimenting with his own life.

Herbert Otto

To laugh is to risk appearing the fool.
To weep is to risk appearing sentimental.
To reach out to another is to risk involvement.
To expose your feelings is to risk exposing yourself.
To place your ideas and your dreams before the crowd
is to risk ridicule.
But risks must be taken, because the greatest risk in life
is to risk nothing.
The person who risks nothing,
does nothing, has nothing, and is nothing.
He may avoid suffering and sorrow,
but he simply cannot learn to feel,
and to grow and to love and to live.
Chained by his certitudes, he is a slave.
Only the person who risks is truly free.

Anonymous

 WHAT IS THE BIGGEST RISK
YOU'VE EVER TAKEN?
WAS IT WORTH IT?

The only thing one never regrets is one's mistakes.

Oscar Wilde

Believe me!
The secret of reaping the greatest fruitfulness
and the greatest enjoyment from life
is to live dangerously!

Friedrich Nietzsche

I must tell you I take terrible risks.
Because my playing is very clear,
when I make a mistake you hear it.
If you want me to play only the notes
without specific dynamics,
I will never make one mistake.
Never be afraid to dare.

Vladimir Horowitz

 ARE YOU READY TO ABANDON YOUR
HOPELESS SEARCH FOR SECURITY?

We cannot become what we need to be
by remaining what we are.

Max De Pree

Twenty years from now you will be
more disappointed by the things you didn't do
than by the ones you did do.
So throw off the bow-lines.
Sail away from the safe harbor.
Catch the trade winds in your sails.
Explore. Dream. Discover.

Anonymous

It is not because things are difficult
that we do not dare;
it is because we do not dare
that they are difficult.

Seneca

 IS IT POSSIBLE TO LIVE LIFE TO THE FULLEST
WITHOUT FILLING YOUR LIFE WITH RISKS?

Without love
the acquisition of knowledge
only increases confusion and leads to self-destruction.

J. Krishnamurti

He not busy being born is busy dying.

Bob Dylan

We must always change, renew,
rejuvenate ourselves;
otherwise we harden.

Johann von Goethe

 IF YOU DIDN'T KNOW
HOW OLD YOU WERE,
HOW OLD WOULD YOU BE?

One learns through the heart,
not the eyes or the intellect.

Mark Twain

Rest not! Life is sweeping by;
go and dare before you die.

Johann von Goethe

Danger and delight grow on one stalk.

English proverb

34

Education is not filling a bucket
but
the lighting of a fire.

William Butler Yeats

He who asks of life nothing but
the improvement of his own nature…
is less liable than anyone else
to miss and waste life.

General Henri Frederic Amiel

 WHAT ONE LIFE EXPERIENCE
HAS TAUGHT YOU THE MOST?

There is no meaning to life
except the meaning man gives to his life
by the unfolding
of his powers.

Erich Fromm

There are periods when to dare is the highest wisdom.

William Ellery Channing

35

To be nobody-but-yourself—
in a world which is doing its best night and day,
to make you everybody else—
means to fight the hardest battle
which anybody can fight; and never stop fighting.

e.e. cummings

 WHAT WOULD YOU LIKE
TO BE REMEMBERED FOR?

It is our love that fashions us into
the fullness of our being—
not our looks, not our work, not our wants,
not our achievements, not our parents,
not our status, not our dreams.
These are all the fodder and the filler,
the navigating of our lives;
but it is love,
who we love, how we love,
why we love and that we love
which ultimately shapes our lives.

Daphne Rose Kingma

Our deepest fear is not that we are inade
Our deepest fear is that we are
powerful beyond measure.
It is our light, not our darkness,
that frightens us most.
We ask ourselves,
who am I to be brilliant, gorgeous, talented and fabulous?
Actually who are you not to be?
You are a child of the universe.
We were born to manifest the glory of the universe
that is within us.
It's not just in some of us; it's in everyone.

Marianne Williamson

 WHAT IS THE PREFECT MOMENT TO BEGIN
MANIFESTING ALL OF YOUR POWER?

Man's main task is to give birth to himself,
to become what he potentially is.
The most important product of his effort is
his own personality.

Erich Fromm

Keep me away from
the wisdom that does not cry,
the philosophy that does not laugh and
the greatness that does not bow before children.

Kahlil Gibran

What is alive, and open, and active,
is good.
All that makes for inertia, lifelessness, dreariness,
is bad.
This is the essence of morality.

D.H. Lawrence

 IS YOUR LIFE ALIVE OR BAD?

In every community,
there is work to be done.
In every nation,
there are wounds to heal.
In every heart there is power to do it.

Marianne Williamson

HAPPINESS

When some external event raises your spirits,
and you think good days are preparing for you,
do not believe it.
It can never be so.
Nothing can bring you peace but yourself.

Ralph Waldo Emerson

One of the hardest lessons
we have to learn in this life,
and one that many persons never learn,
is to see the divine, the celestial,
the pure in the common, the near at hand—
to see that heaven lies about us in this world.

John Burroughs

The ideals which have lighted my way,
and time after time have given me
new courage to face life cheerfully,
have been Kindness, Beauty, and Truth…
The trite subjects of human efforts—
possessions, outward success, luxury—
have always seemed contemptible.

Albert Einstein

 WHAT IS THE MOST BEAUTIFUL SIGHT
YOU HAVE EVER SEEN?

Happiness is good health and a bad memory.

Ingrid Bergman

It is an illusion to think that more comfort
means more happiness.
Happiness comes of the capacity to feel deeply,
to enjoy simply, to think freely,
to be needed.

Storm Jameson

 WHAT IS THE ONE SECRET TO HAPPINESS
YOU ARE ABSOLUTELY SURE OF?

True happiness flows from the possession
of wisdom and virtue
and not from the possession of external goods.

Aristotle

Between the house and the store
are little pockets of happiness.
A bird, a garden, a child's smile,
a cat in the sunshine needing a stroke.
Recognize them or ignore them.
It's always up to you.

Pam Brown

41

Happiness does not consist in having what you want,
but wanting what you have.

Confucius

The art of being happy lies in the power of
extracting happiness from common things.

Henry Ward Beecher

If you can spend a perfectly useless afternoon
in a perfectly useless manner,
you have learned how to live.

Lin Yu-tang

 CAN YOU SIT IN THE SUN,
WATCHING THE CHILDREN PLAY,
LISTENING TO THE BIRDS SING,
KNOWING THERE IS NOTHING MORE TO DO?

Fear less, hope more; eat less, chew more;
whine less, breathe more; talk less, say more;
love more and all good things will be yours.

Swedish proverb

Happiness in this world, when it comes, comes incidently.
Make it the object of pursuit,
and it leads us on a wild-goose chase,
and is never attained.
Follow some other object,
and very possibly we may find that
we have caught happiness without dreaming of it.
Nathaniel Hawthorne

If you observe a really happy man,
you'll find him building a boat,
writing a symphony,
educating his son,
growing dahlias,
or looking for dinosaur eggs in the Gobi Desert.
He will not be searching for happiness as if it were
a collar button that had rolled under the radiator,
striving for it as a goal in itself.
He will have become aware that he is happy
in the course of living life
twenty-four hours of each day.
W. Beran Wolfe

43

The happiness of life is made up of minute fractions—
the little, soon-forgotten charities of a kiss or smile,
a kind look, a heart-felt compliment,
and the countless infinitesimals of pleasurable
and genial feeling.

Samuel Taylor Coleridge

 DO YOU SPEND MORE OF YOUR TIME
SEARCHING FOR HAPPINESS
THAN CREATING IT?

The best things are the nearest:
breath in your nostrils,
light in your eyes,
flowers at your feet,
duties in your hand,
the path of God just before you.
Then do not grasp at the stars but do life's
plain, common work as it comes,
certain that daily duties and daily bread
are the sweetest things in life.

Robert Louis Stevenson

We who lived in concentration camps can remember
the men who walked through the huts
comforting others,
giving away their last piece of bread.
They may have been few in number,
but they offer sufficient proof that everything
can be taken away from a man but one thing:
the last of the human freedoms—
to choose one's attitude
in any given set of circumstances,
to choose one's own way.

Viktor Frankl

 IS YOUR HAPPINESS A PRESENT ATTITUDE,
OR A FUTURE CONDITION?

If happiness truly consisted in physical ease
and freedom from care,
then the happiest individual…
would be, I think,
an American cow.

William Lyon Phelps

Nine requisites for contented living:
Health enough to make work a pleasure.
Wealth enough to support your needs.
Strength to battle with difficulties
and overcome them.
Grace enough to confess your sins
and forsake them.
Patience enough to make real the things of God.
Charity enough to see some good in your neighbor.
Love enough to move you to be helpful.
Faith enough to make real the things of God.
Hope enough to remove all anxious fears
concerning the future.

Johann von Goethe

One is happy as a result of one's own efforts—
once one knows the necessary ingredients
of happiness: simple tastes,
a certain degree of courage,
self-denial to a point, love of work,
and, above all, a clear conscience.

George Sand

I looked for happiness in fast living,
but it was not there.
I tried to find it in money,
but it was not there, either.
But when I placed myself in tune with what
I believe to be the fundamental truths of life,
when I began to develop my limited ability,
to rid my mind of kinds of tangled thoughts
and fill it with zeal and courage and love,
when I gave myself a chance by treating myself
decently and sensibly,
I began to feel the stimulating, warm glow of
happiness.

Edward Young

 SHOULD YOUR HAPPINESS BE DEPENDENT
UPON OTHERS AND EXTERNAL CONDITIONS,
OR SHOULD IT BE UNCONDITIONAL?

There are three ingredients in the good life:
learning, earning, and yearning.

Christopher Morley

MAGNIFICENT KINDNESS

Kindness is more important than wisdom,
and the recognition of this
is the beginning of wisdom.

Theodore Isaac Rubin

The world is in desperate need of human beings
whose level of growth is sufficient to enable them
to live and work with others cooperatively and lovingly,
to care for others—
not for what those others can do for you
or what they think of you,
but rather in terms of what you can do for them.
Elisabeth Kübler-Ross

What matters is that we recognize
our smallness in the universe and see
kindness
as the only avenue towards a larger self.
Gloria Wade-Gayles

If you help others, you will be helped,
perhaps tomorrow, perhaps in one hundred years,
but you will be helped.
Nature must pay off the debt...
It's a mathematical law
and all life is mathematics.

Gurdjieff

Be kind—everyone you meet is fighting a hard battle.

John Watson

If someone comes to you asking for help,
do not say in refusal, "Trust in God, he will help."
Rather, act as if there were no God,
and no one to help except you.

Zaddik

 IS THERE ANY WISDOM THAT IS
GREATER THAN KINDNESS?

It is one of the most beautiful compensations of life
that no man can sincerely try
to help another
without helping himself.

Ralph Waldo Emerson

... When your thinking rises above concern
for your own welfare,
wisdom which is independent of thought appears.

Ha Gakure

If you want happiness for an hour,
take a nap.
If you want happiness for a day,
go fishing.
If you want happiness for a month,
get married.
If you want happiness for a year,
inherit a fortune.
If you want happiness for a lifetime,
help someone else.

Chinese proverb

 WHAT IS THE KINDEST THING
YOU'VE EVER DONE FOR SOMEONE?

I believe that man will not merely endure; he will prevail.
He is immortal,
not because he alone among the creatures
has an inexhaustible voice,
but because he has a soul,
a spirit capable of kindness and compassion.

William Faulkner

51

The best portion of a good man's life—
his little, nameless, unremembered acts
of kindness and of love.

William Wordsworth

When I was young I admired clever people.
Now that I am old, I admire kind people.

Abraham Joshua Heschel

Kindness in words creates confidence.
Kindness in thinking creates profoundness.
Kindness in giving creates love.

Lao-tzu

 GIVEN A CHOICE, IS IT BETTER TO BE KIND
OR TO BE HONEST?

Tenderness and kindness
are not signs of weakness and despair
but
manifestations of strength and resolution.

Kahlil Gibran

What you deny to others will be denied to you,
for the plain reason that
you are always legislating for yourself;
all your words and actions define the world you want to live in.

Thaddeus Golas

My religion is very simple.
My religion is kindness.

The Dalai Lama

Every being is your counterpart.
Every other human being possesses
and embodies aspects of yourself:
your dreams, your sorrows,
your hope that life will not turn out to be a dirty joke.
Therefore we are all quite alike;
indeed at the core we are all one, all lost—and found—
in a mysterious enterprise that is life.
Hold this in your heart as you go about your day,
and the world will cease to be inhabited by strangers,
and the burden of love itself will
no longer be a process of loneliness.

Daphne Rose Kingma

Each person has inside a basic decency and goodness.
If he listens to it and acts on it,
he is giving a great deal of what the world needs most.
It is not complicated but it takes courage.
It takes courage for a person to
listen to his own goodness and act on it.

Pablo Casals

The weak can never forgive.
Forgiveness is the attribute of the strong.

Mahatma Gandhi

 WHY IS FORGIVENESS A SELFISH ACT?

Forgiveness is the answer to the child's
dream of a miracle by which
what is broken is made whole again,
what is soiled is again made clean.

Dag Hammarskjöld

Only a life lived for others is worth living.

Albert Einstein

PURPOSE

Perhaps it would be a good idea,
fantastic as it sounds,
to muffle every telephone, stop every motor
and halt all activity for an hour some day
to give people a chance to
ponder for a few minutes on what it is all about,
why are they living and what they really want.

James Truslow Adams

Life is no "brief candle" to me.
It is a sort of splendid torch
which I've got a hold on for the moment,
and I want to make it burn as brightly as possible
before handing it on
to future generations.

George Bernard Shaw

 WHAT WILL YOUR LEGACY BE?
AND HOW FAR ALONG ARE YOU?

When you are inspired by some great purpose,
some extraordinary project,
all your thoughts break their bonds,
your mind transcends limitations,
your consciousness expands in every direction,
and you find yourself in a
new great and wonderful world.
Dormant forces, faculties and talents become alive,
and you find yourself to be a greater person by far
than you ever dreamed yourself to be.

Patanjali

Nurture your minds with great thoughts.
To believe in the heroic makes heroes.

Benjamin Disraeli

It is the paradox of life that
the way to miss pleasure is to seek it first.
The very condition of lasting happiness is that
a life should be full of purpose,
aiming at something outside self.

Hugh Black

 WHAT ONE THING WOULD YOU LIKE TO
ACCOMPLISH BEFORE YOU DIE?

Learn to get in touch with the silence within yourself
and know that everything in this life has a purpose.

Elisabeth Kübler-Ross

The whole meaning of our existence
and the consuming desire of the heart of God
is that we should let ourselves be loved.

Ruth Burrows

57

Great minds have purposes;
others have wishes.

Washington Irving

 WHAT IS YOUR SPECIAL GIFT TO
THE FAMILY OF THE WORLD?

Inspiration may be a form of superconsciousness,
or perhaps subconsciousness—
I wouldn't know.
But I am sure it is the antithesis of self-consciousness.

Aaron Copland

Service is the rent we pay for being.
It is the very purpose of life and
not something you do in your spare time.

Marian Wright Edelman

 HOW RICH WOULD YOU BE TOMORROW,
IF YOU LOST EVERY DOLLAR YOU HAVE?

Superfluous wealth can buy superfluities only.
Money is not required to buy one necessity of the soul.
Henry David Thoreau

The purpose of our life usually
has something to do with
learning how to love
more fully,
more deeply,
more constantly,
more unconditionally.
Carol Adrienne

 BESIDES SATISFYING YOUR PERSONAL NEEDS,
WHAT IS THE PURPOSE OF FRIENDSHIP?

You are born with a character;
it is given, a gift,
as the old stories say,
from the guardians upon your birth…
Each person enters the world called.
James Hillman

Do not care overly much for wealth
or power or fame,
or one day you will meet someone
who cares for none of these things,
and you will realize
how poor you have become.

Rudyard Kipling

 YOU ARE HERE TO DO SOMETHING—
WHAT IS IT?

In the lives of many people
it is possible to find a unifying purpose
that justifies the things they do
day in, day out—
a goal that like a magnetic field
attracts their psychic energy,
a goal upon which all lesser goals depend...
Without such a purpose,
even the best-ordered consciousness
lacks meaning.

Mihaly Csikszentmihalyi

W_{hen} this new type of commitment starts to operate,
there is a flow around us.
Things just seem to happen.
We begin to see that with very small movements,
at just the right time and place,
all sorts of consequent actions are brought into being.
We develop what artists refer to as
"an economy of means," where,
rather than getting things done
through effort and brute force,
we start to operate very subtly.
A flow of meaning begins to operate around us,
as if we were a part of a larger conversation.

Peter Senge

 WHAT WERE YOU DOING
WHEN YOU FELT "IN THE FLOW"?

A_{gain} and again the sacred texts tell us that our life purpose
is to understand and develop the power of spirit,
power that is vital to our mental and physical well-being.

Caroline Myss

I believe happiness and joy are the purpose of life.
If we know that the future will be very dark or painful,
then we lose our determination to live.
Therefore, life is something based on hope.
…An innate quality among sentient beings,
particularly among human beings,
is the urge or strong feeling
to encounter or experience happiness
and discard suffering or pain.
Therefore, the whole basis of human life
is the experience of different levels of happiness.
Achieving or experiencing happiness
is the purpose of life.

The Dalai Lama

It's not enough to say,
"I'm earning enough to live and support my family.
I do my work well. I'm a good father.
I'm a good churchgoer."
That's all very well
but you must do something more.

Albert Schweitzer

IF YOU WERE TO FINISH THE SENTENCE
"MY LIFE PURPOSE IS..., HOW WOULD IT END?

Just when I found out the meaning of life,
they changed it.

George Carlin

No trumpets sound when
the important decisions of our life are made.
Destiny is made known silently.

Agnes de Mille

A life of value is not a series of great things well done;
it is a series of small things consciously done.

Joan Chittister

When we are in this state of being where
we are open to all life and all its possibilities,
willing to take the next step as it is presented to us,
then we meet the most remarkable people
who are important contributors to our life.

Joseph Jaworski

Every situation has a purpose.
Doing what you love aligns you with
the flow of synchronicity.
You attract what you focus on.
Universal intelligence is perfect and operates effortlessly.
You always have a choice.
Set your intention and ask for support.
Let the universe handle the details.
Trust the process.
Your life is part of the larger world plan.

Carol Adrienne

 SHOULD ALL YOUR DECISIONS BE
BASED UPON YOUR PURPOSE?

I discovered that people are not really afraid of dying;
they're afraid of not ever having lived,
not ever having deeply considered
their life's higher purpose,
and not ever having stepped into that purpose
and at least tried to make a difference in the world.

Joseph Jaworski

GRATITUDE

I dance not to get better
nor to fix myself,
I dance to remember
that I am not sick.

Malidoma Some

In ordinary life we hardly realize that
we receive a great deal more than we give,
and that it is only with gratitude
that life becomes rich.

Dietrich Bonhoeffer

 IS THERE ANYONE TO WHOM
YOU NEED TO SAY "THANK YOU"?

If the only prayer you say in your whole life
is "thank you," that would suffice.

Meister Eckhart

Gratitude is not only the greatest of virtues,
but the mother of all the rest.

Cicero

I thank You God most for this amazing
day for the leaping greenly spirits of trees
and a blue true dream of sky, and for everything
which is natural which is infinite which is yes.

e.e. cummings

The more you praise and celebrate your life,
the more there is in life to celebrate.
The more you complain,
the more you find fault,
the more misery and fault you will have to find.
                    Oprah Winfrey

The one sure way to become instantly happy is to
spend a day at the intensive care unit of a hospital.
                    Anonymous

 IS IT POSSIBLE TO FEEL DEPRESSED
AND GRATEFUL AT THE SAME TIME?

We have no right to ask when a sorrow comes,
"Why did this happen to me?"
unless we ask the same question
for every joy that comes our way.
                    Philip Bernstein

Wisdom is seeing the miraculous in the common.
                    Ralph Waldo Emerson

67

We do not see things as they are.
We see them as we are.

The Talmud

 CAN THE FEELING OF GRATITUDE
RELIEVE YOUR OWN INNER SUFFERING?

If you see suffering all around you,
it is just a reflection of your own inner suffering.
If you want to alleviate suffering, go to the root cause
which is the suffering inside yourself.

Annamalai Swami

We all experience "soul moments" in life—
when we see a magnificent sunrise,
hear the call of the loon,
see the wrinkles in our mother's hands,
or smell the sweetness of a baby.
During these moments, our body,
as well as our brain, resonates as we experience
the glory of being a human being.

Marion Woodman

68

About ninety percent of the things in our lives
are right and about ten percent are wrong.
If we want to be happy, all we have to do
is to concentrate on the ninety percent that are right
and ignore the ten percent that are wrong.

Dale Carnegie

There are only two ways to live your life.
One is as though nothing is a miracle.
The other is as though everything is a miracle.

Albert Einstein

 DOES UNEXPRESSED GRATITUDE
HAVE ANY VALUE?

The little things? The little moments?
They aren't little.

Jon Kabat-Zinn

Your daily life is your temple and your religion.
Whenever you enter into it, take with you your all.

Kahlil Gibran

The moment one gives attention to anything,
even a blade of grass,
it becomes a mysterious, awesome,
indescribably magnificent world in itself.

Henry Miller

A person will be called on Judgement Day
for every permissible thing he might have enjoyed
but did not.

The Talmud

 WHAT IS THE VALUE OF ONE MOMENT OF JOY,
IF A DYING PERSON CANNOT BUY IT WITH
ALL THE MONEY IN THE WORLD?

To be happy is easy enough if we give ourselves,
forgive others, and live with thanksgiving.
No self-centered person,
no ungrateful soul can ever be happy,
much less make anyone else happy.
Life is giving, not getting.

Joseph Fort Newton

Millions long for immortality who don't know
what to do with themselves
on a rainy Sunday afternoon.

Susan Ertz

 WHICH ONE OF YOUR UNIQUE TALENTS
ARE YOU MOST GRATEFUL FOR?

People usually consider
walking on water or in thin air a miracle.
But I think the real miracle is not to walk
either on water or in thin air, but to walk on earth.
Every day we are engaged in a miracle
which we don't even recognize: a blue sky,
white clouds, green leaves,
the black curious eyes of a child—our own two eyes.
All is a miracle.

Thich Nhat Hanh

 WHO ARE YOU MOST GRATEFUL FOR?

Ryokan, a Zen master, lived the simplest kind of life in a little hut at the foot of a mountain. One evening a thief entered the hut only to discover there was nothing to steal.

Ryokan returned and caught him. "You may have come a long way to visit me," he told the prowler, "and you should not return empty-handed. Please take my clothes as a gift."

The thief was bewildered. He took the clothes and slunk away.

Ryokan sat naked, watching the moon. "Poor fellow," he mused, "I wish I could give him this beautiful moon."

Zen teacher, Muju

To the poet, to the philosopher, to the saint,
all things are friendly and sacred,
all events profitable,
all days holy, all men divine.

Ralph Waldo Emerson

My soul can find no staircase to Heaven
unless it be through Earth's loveliness.

Michelangelo

SERVING OTHERS

Strange as it may seem,
life becomes serene and enjoyable
precisely when selfish pleasure
and personal success
are no longer the guiding goals.
                    Mihaly Csikszentmihalyi

The sole meaning of life is to serve humanity.
Leo Tolstoy

A man's value to the community primarily depends on
how far his feelings, thoughts, and actions are
directed towards promoting the good of his fellows.
Albert Einstein

 IS HAPPINESS POSSIBLE WITHOUT
SERVING SOMEONE?

Make the decision to serve
wherever you go
and whomever you see.
As long as you are serving,
you will be receiving and
the more confidence you will gain
in the miraculous effects
of this principle of life.
And as you enjoy the reciprocity,
your ability to serve will also increase.
Greg Anderson

I don't know what your destiny will be,
but one thing I do know:
the only ones among you
who will be truly happy
are those who have
sought and found
how to serve.

Albert Schweitzer

 WHAT ARE THE NEGATIVE RESULTS
OF SERVING OTHERS?

If you cannot feed a hundred people,
then feed just one.

Mother Teresa

I know some good marriages—
marriages where both people are just
trying to get through their days by
helping each other,
being good to each other.

Erica Jong

75

To serve is beautiful,
but only if it is done with joy
and a whole heart
and a free mind.

Pearl S. Buck

 IF NOT FOR MAKING LIFE LESS DIFFICULT
FOR OTHERS, WHAT DO WE LIVE FOR?

The quality of mercy is not strained;
It droppeth as the gentle rain from heaven
Upon the place beneath.
It is twice blessed—
It blesseth him that gives and him that takes.

Shakespeare

People who won't help others in trouble
"because they got into trouble through their own fault"
would probably not throw a lifeline
to a drowning man until they learned
whether he fell in through his own fault or not.

Sydney Harris

To laugh often and love much;
To win the respect of intelligent people
and the affection of children;
To earn the approbation of honest critics
and endure the betrayal of false friends;
To appreciate beauty;
To find the best in others;
To leave the world a bit better,
whether by a healthy child,
a redeemed social condition,
or a job well done;
To have played
and worked with enthusiasm
and sung with exultation;
To know even one life
has breathed easier
because you have lived—
This is to have succeeded.

Ralph Waldo Emerson

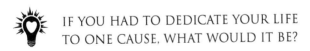 IF YOU HAD TO DEDICATE YOUR LIFE
TO ONE CAUSE, WHAT WOULD IT BE?

Happiness cannot come from without.
It must come from within.
It is not what we see and touch
or that which others do for us
which makes us happy;
it is that which we think and feel and do,
first for the other fellow and then for ourselves.

Helen Keller

The most infectious, joyous men and women
are those who forget themselves
in thinking about others
and serving others.

Robert J. McCracken

Try to forget yourself in the service of others.
For when we think too much of ourselves
and our own interests,
we easily become despondent.
But when we work for others,
our efforts return to bless us.

Sidney Powell

COMPASSION

If you want *others* to be happy,
practice compassion.
If *you* want to be happy,
practice compassion.

The Dalai Lama

I feel the capacity to care
is the thing which gives life
its deepest significance and meaning.

Pablo Casals

Compassion is the basis of all truthful relationship:
it means being present with love—
for ourselves and for all life,
including animals,
fish,
birds,
and trees.

Ram Dass

 CAN YOU HAVE COMPASSION FOR OTHERS
WITHOUT HAVING COMPASSION
FOR YOURSELF?

I never ask a wounded person how he feels;
I myself
become the wounded person.

Walt Whitman

WHO HAS TAUGHT YOU THE MOST
ABOUT COMPASSION?

Compassion is...a spirituality and a way of
living and walking through life.
It is the way we treat all there is in life—
ourselves, our bodies, our imaginations and dreams,
our neighbors, our enemies...
Compassion is a spirituality as if creation mattered.
It is treating all creation as holy and as divine...
Which is what it is.

Matthew Fox

It is through compassion that a person achieves
the highest peak and deepest reach
in his or her search for self-fulfillment.

Arthur Jersild

Tell me how much you know
of the sufferings of your fellow men
and I will tell you how much you have loved them.

Helmut Thielicke

How far you go in life depends on your being
tender with the young,
compassionate with the aged,
sympathetic with the striving,
and tolerant of the weak and strong.
Because someday in life
you will have been all of these.

George Washington Carver

 IS IT POSSIBLE TO BE COMPASSIONATE
IN EVERY SITUATION?

Compassion means to lay a bridge over to the other
without knowing whether he wants to be reached.

Henri J.M. Nouwen

The whole idea of compassion is based on
a keen awareness of the interdependence
of all these living beings,
which are all part of one another
and all involved in one another.

Thomas Merton

By compassion we make others' misery our own,
and so,
by relieving them,
we relieve ourselves also.

Sir Thomas Browne

 WHAT IS THE VALUE OF YOUR COMPASSION
IF YOU ARE NOT MOTIVATED TO ACT?

When we quit thinking primarily of ourselves
and our own self-preservation,
we undergo a truly
heroic transformation of consciousness.

Joseph Campbell

True compassion is not just an emotional response,
but a firm commitment founded on reason.
Therefore,
a truly compassionate attitude toward others
does not change,
even if they behave negatively.

The Dalai Lama

83

TAKING ACTION

I don't sing because I'm happy;
I'm happy because I sing.

William James

Even the most enlightened beings,
even the holiest saints, make mistakes.
But whereas foolish people cover up their mistakes
and keep on making the same ones,
the wise correct their mistakes
and never make the same ones twice.
The ability to correct our mistakes and to change ourselves
is called wisdom.

Anonymous

If you can find a path with no obstacles,
it probably doesn't lead anywhere.

Frank Clark

If a man has a talent and cannot use it,
he has failed.
If he has a talent and uses only part of it,
he has partly failed.
If he has talent and somehow manages to use the whole of it,
he has gloriously succeeded,
and won a satisfaction that few men ever know.

Thomas Wolfe

85

Nothing would be done at all
if we waited until we could do it so well
that no one could find fault with it.

John Henry Newman

Men acquire a particular quality by
constantly acting in a particular way…
We become just by performing just actions,
Temperate by performing temperate actions,
brave by performing brave actions.

Aristotle

 WHICH IS OF MORE VALUE,
A GREAT THOUGHT OR
A THOUGHTFUL ACTION?

What we think, or what we know,
or what we believe, is in the end,
of little consequence.
The only thing of consequence is
what we do.

John Ruskin

Thousands of people have talent.
I might as well congratulate you
for having eyes in your head.
The one and only thing that counts is:
Do you have staying power?

Noël Coward

There is no such thing as a problem
without a gift in its hands.
You seek problems because you need their gifts.

Richard Bach

 IF PROBLEMS BRING GIFTS,
WHAT SHOULD THEY BE CALLED?

Bless a thing and it will bless you.
Curse it and it will curse you…
If you bless a situation,
it has no power to hurt you,
and even if it is troublesome for a time,
it will gradually fade out, if you sincerely bless it.

Emmet Fox

When I hear someone say,
"Life is hard,"
I am always tempted to ask,
"Compared to what?"

Sydney Harris

The man with the clear head is the man who...
looks life in the face,
realizes that everything in it is problematic,
and feels himself lost.
And it is the simple truth:
that to live is to feel oneself lost.

Jose Ortega y Gasset

Whatever course you decide upon,
there is always someone to tell you that you are wrong.
There are always difficulties arising
which tempt you to believe your critics are right.
To map out a course of action
and follow it to an end requires...
courage.

Ralph Waldo Emerson

When you get in a tight place
and everything goes against you,
'til it seems as though you
could not hold on a minute longer,
never give up then,
for that is just the place and time that
the tide will turn.

Harriet Beecher Stowe

 WHEN YOU PLAN TO SUCCEED,
ARE YOU ALSO PREPARED TO FAIL?

All life is an experiment.
The more experiments you make,
the better.
What if they are a little coarse,
and you may get your coat soiled or torn?
What if you do fail,
and get fairly rolled in the dirt once or twice?
Up again,
you shall never be so afraid to tumble.

Ralph Waldo Emerson

Here is my lesson from the heavy rain:
on your way, you meet a shower.
You dislike to get wet,
so you hurry along the streets running under eaves.
Still, you get wet all the same.
As long as you accept that you will get wet,
you won't suffer from being wet.

Minoru Tanaka

 IF YOU COULD FOREVER ELIMINATE
ONE OF YOUR FEARS,
WHICH ONE WOULD IT BE?

Courage is not the absence of fear,
but rather the judgment that something else is
more important than fear.

Ambrose Redmoon

A good plan vigorously executed right now
is far better than a
perfect plan executed next week.

General George Patton

The highest courage is not to be found in
the instinctive acts of men who risk their lives
to save a friend or slay a foe;
the physical fearlessness of a moment or an hour
is not to be compared with the immolation of
months or years for the sake of wisdom or art.

Joseph H. Odell

 WHAT WOULD HAPPEN TO YOUR LIFE
IF YOU HAD THE COURAGE TO
PURSUE ANYTHING?

The only way to get positive feelings about yourself
is to take positive actions.
Man does not live as he thinks,
he thinks as he lives.

Vaughan Quinn

Take your life into your own hands
and what happens?
A terrible thing: no one to blame.

Erica Jong

When nothing seems to help
I go and look at the stonecutter hammering away at his rock
perhaps a hundred times
without so much as a crack showing in it.
Yet at the hundred and first blow it will split in two,
and I know it was not that blow that did it—
but all that had gone before.

Jacob Riis

Nothing in the world can take the place of persistence.
Talent will not;
nothing is more common
than unsuccessful people with talent.
Genius will not;
unrewarded genius is almost a proverb.
Education will not;
the world is full of educated derelicts.
Persistence and determination are alone supreme.

Calvin Coolidge

One day as a tiger is better than a thousand as a sheep.

Alison Hargreaves

Most people never run far enough on their first wind
to find out they've got a second.
Give your dreams all you've got
and you'll be amazed at the energy
that comes out of you.

William James

 WHAT ARE YOU GETTING READY TO
GET READY TO DO?

Hope is an orientation of the spirit,
an orientation of the heart.
It is not the conviction that something
will turn out well,
but the certainty that something makes sense,
regardless of how it turns out.

Vaclav Havel

I cannot give you the formula for success,
but I can give you the formula for failure—which is:
Try to please everybody.

Bill Cosby

In the archer there is a resemblance to
the mature person.
When he misses the bull's-eye,
he turns and seeks the reason for his failure
in himself.

Confucius

As I grow older,
I pay less attention to what men say.
I just watch what they do.

Andrew Carnegie

Trust in God and do something.

Mary Lyon

It is not only what we do, but also what we do not do,
for which we are accountable.

Molière

A life spent making mistakes is
not only more honorable but more useful than
a life spent doing nothing.

George Bernard Shaw

Every kind of work can be a pleasure.
Even simple household tasks can be an opportunity
to exercise and expand our caring,
our effectiveness,
our responsiveness.
As we respond with caring and vision to all work,
we develop our capacity to respond fully to all of life.
Every action generates energy
which can be shared with others.
These qualities of caring and responsiveness
are the greatest gift we can offer.

Tarthang Tulku

Perhaps the most valuable result of all education
is the ability to make yourself do the thing you have to do
when it ought to done,
whether you like it or not;
it is the first lesson that ought to be learned;
however early a man's training begins,
it is probably the last lesson
he learns thoroughly.

Thomas Henry Huxley

95

If I had my life to live over again,
I'd make more mistakes next time.
I would relax.
I'd be sillier than I have been on this trip.
I would climb more mountains,
swim more rivers and watch more sunsets.
I would have more actual troubles
and less imaginary ones.
Oh, I've had my moments,
and if I had to do it over again,
I'd have more of them.
In fact, I'd try to have nothing else,
just moments, one after another...

Nadine Stair

 IF YOU HAD ONE REGRET,
WHAT WOULD IT BE?

As you grow older,
you'll find the only regrets
are the things you didn't do.

Zachary Scott

Many years ago a very wise man named
Bernard Baruch took me aside and put his arm around
my shoulder.
"Harpo my boy," he said, "I'm going to give
you three pieces of advice you should always
remember."
My heart jumped and I glowed with expectation.
I was going to hear the magic password to a rich, full
life from the master himself.
"Yes sir?" I said.
And he told me three things.
I regret that I've forgotten what they were.

Harpo Marx

 WHO WILL GET TO HEAVEN FIRST,
THE PERSON WHO THINKS,
THE PERSON WHO TALKS,
OR THE PERSON WHO ACTS?

Action may not bring happiness,
but there is no happiness without action.

William James

THE SPIRITUAL PATH

If one wants to enter a spiritual path,
to explore soul,
a certain warrior quality is needed.
I'm not speaking of defeating someone,
but of having a courageous heart.

Jack Kornfield

God is love.
And in every moment of genuine love
we are dwelling in God and God in us.

Paul Tillich

 IS GOD MORE THAN LOVE?

One of the hardest lessons we have to learn in this life,
and one that many persons never learn,
is to see the divine, the celestial,
the pure in the common, the near at hand—
to see that heaven lies about us here in this world.

John Burroughs

The scientist's religious feeling takes the form of
a rapturous amazement at the harmony of natural law,
which reveals an intelligence of such superiority
that, in comparison with it,
the highest intelligence of human beings is
an utterly insignificant reflection.
This feeling is the guiding principle of his life and work.

Albert Einstein

99

Prayer takes place in the heart, not the head.

Carlo Carretto

We don't have all the answers.
Perhaps prayer is simply a time we set aside
to acknowledge that reality.

Mary E. Hunt

Prayer is naught else but a yearning of soul…
It draws down the great God
into the little heart;
it brings together these two lovers,
God and the soul,
in a wondrous place
where they can speak of love.

Mechthild of Magdeburg

 WHAT IS MORE POWERFUL:
TO PRAY FOR SOMEONE OR TO HELP THEM?

No man has ever prayed without learning something.

Ralph Waldo Emerson

The most simple prayer is honesty and humility.
One can never go wrong with these two.
Talk honestly to God.
Don't give God the self you think you're supposed to be.
Give God yourself in your nakedness,
who you really are,
even if that means giving God your anger or distractions.

Richard Rohr

 IS PRAYER YOUR COMPASS
OR YOUR LIFE PRESERVER?

Prayer is not a stratagem for occasional use.
A refuge to resort to now and then.
It is rather like an established residence
for the innermost self.
All things have a home:
the bird has a nest,
the fox has a hole,
the bee has a hive.
A soul without prayer is a soul without a home.

Abraham Joshua Heschel

If a care is too small to be turned into a prayer,
it is too small to be make into a burden.

Corrie ten Boom

 IS FAITH A NOUN OR A VERB?

Doubt is not the opposite of faith;
it is one element of faith.

Paul Tillich

Everything that God created is potentially holy,
and our task as humans is to find that holiness
in seemingly unholy situations.
When we can do this,
we will have learned to nurture our souls.

Harold Kushner

Awe precedes faith;
it is the root of faith.
We must grow in awe
in order to reach faith.

Abraham Joshua Heschel

Faith strips the mask from the world and
reveals God in everything.
It makes nothing impossible and
renders meaningless such words as anxiety, danger,
and fear, so that the believer goes through life calmly
and peacefully, with profound joy—like a child,
hand in hand with his mother.

Charles de Foucauld

 WHAT WAS THE MOST
SPIRITUAL EXPERIENCE OF YOUR LIFE?

When you realize where you come from,
you naturally become tolerant,
disinterested,
amused,
kindhearted as a grandmother,
dignified as a king.
Immersed in the wonder of the Tao,
you can deal with whatever life brings you,
and when death comes, you are ready.

Lao-tzu

God wants nothing from you
but the gift of a peaceful heart.

Meister Eckhart

Love is what we were born with.
Fear is what we learned here.
The spiritual journey is the relinquishment or unlearning
of fear and the acceptance of love back into our hearts.

Marianne Williamson

 ARE THERE EXCEPTIONS TO
DIVINE PERFECTION?

It is not my business to think about myself.
My business is to think about God.
It is for God to think about me.

Simone Weil

And how, you ask, are we to walk the spiritual path?
We answer: say little, and love much; give all;
judge no man; aspire to all that is pure and good.

White Eagle

To accept the responsibility of being a child of God
is to accept the best life has to offer you.

Stella Terrill Mann

 DOES YOUR RELIGION INCLUDE JOY?

In music,
in the sea,
in a flower,
in a leaf,
in an act of kindness…
I see what people call God in all these things.

Pablo Casals

The soul needs an intense, full-bodied spiritual life
as much as and in the same way that
the body needs food.

Thomas Moore

Until you have found God in your soul,
the whole world will seem meaningless to you.

Rabindranath Tagore

Spirituality is an inner fire,
a mystical sustenance that feeds our souls.
The mystical journey drives us into ourselves,
to a sacred flame at our center.
The purpose of the religious experience is to develop
the eyes by which we see this inner flame,
and our capacity to live its mystery.
In its presence, we are warmed and ignited.
When we are too far from the blaze,
we are cold and spiritually lifeless.
We are less than human without that heat.
Our connection to God is life itself.

Marianne Williamson

 IF YOU WANT TO KNOW WHETHER YOU ARE
GROWING SPIRITUALLY, ASK YOURSELF,
"AM I BECOMING MORE LOVING?"

Spiritual life is like a moving sidewalk.
Whether you go with it or spend your whole life
running against it, you're still going to be taken along.

Bernadette Roberts

It is proper to doubt.
Do not be led by holy scriptures,
or by mere logic or inference,
or by appearances,
or by the authority of religious teachers.
But when you realize something is bad for you, give it up.
And when you realize that something is
wholesome and good for you, do it.

The Buddha

The most beautiful experience we can have
is the mysterious.
It is the fundamental emotion which stands
at the cradle of true art and science.
Whoever does not know it and can no longer wonder,
no longer marvel, is as good as dead, and his eyes are dimmed.
It was the experience of mystery—
even if mixed with fear—
that engendered religion.
…in this sense and in this alone,
I am a deeply religious man.

Albert Einstein

107

LIVING
CREATIVELY

Every child is an artist.
The problem is how to remain an artist
once he grows up.

Pablo Picasso

Where the spirit does not work with the hand,
there is no art.

Leonardo da Vinci

What does God do all day long?
God lies in a maternity bed giving birth.

Meister Eckhart

Creativity is seeing something that doesn't exist already.
You need to find out how you can bring it into being
and in that way be a playmate with God.

Michele Shea

 WHAT IS STOPPING YOU FROM EXPRESSING
YOUR CREATIVE SELF?

God is really another artist.
He invented the giraffe and the cat.
He has no real style.
He just goes on trying other things.

Pablo Picasso

No amount of skillful invention can replace
the essential element of imagination.

Edward Hopper

Man unites himself with the world
in the process of creation.

Erich Fromm

 DOES YOUR LIFE IMITATE ART, OR IS IT ART?

To live a creative life,
we must lose our fear of being wrong.

Joseph Chilton Pearce

The human spirit lives on creativity
and dies on conformity and routine.

Vilayat Inayat Khan

In order to create
there must be a dynamic force,
and what force is more potent than love.

Igor Stravinsky

I'll play it first and tell you what it is later.
Miles Davis

The mysterious complexity of our life
is not to be embraced by maxims...
to lace ourselves up in formulas of that sort
is to repress all the divine promptings and inspirations
that spring from growing insight and sympathy.
George Eliot

What moves men of genius,
or rather what inspires their work, is not new ideas,
but their obsession with the idea that
what has already been said
is still not enough.
Eugène Delacroix

Inside there's an artist you don't know about...
Say yes quickly, if you know,
if you've known it from before the beginning
of the universe.
Rumi

Making the simple complicated is commonplace;
making the complicated simple,
awesomely simple,
that's creativity.

Charles Mingus

The whole difference between
construction and creation is exactly this:
that a thing constructed can only be loved
after it is constructed;
but a thing created is loved before it exists.

G.K. Chesterton

 DOES EVERY MOMENT OF EVERY DAY
OFFER YOU A CREATIVE OPPORTUNITY?
WHAT DO YOU CREATE?

Creativity can solve any problem.
The creative act,
the defeat of habit by originality,
overcomes everything.

George Lois

Maintaining an attitude of playfulness
may at first seem inappropriate for problem-solving,
but intuitive problem-solving
is basically a creative process,
and is more easily activated when
critical judgement is suspended.

Francis E. Vaughan

We could make our lives so much more interesting,
and develop so many new capacities,
if we sought to work with the unknowns of emergence,
rather than try and plan surprises out of our lives.

Margaret Wheatley

 DO YOU EMBRACE THE ADVENTURE
OF THE SURPRISES?

The creation of the world is not only a process
which moves from God to humanity.
God demands newness from humanity;
God awaits the works of human freedom.

Nicholai Berdyaev

YOUR COMPELLING VISION

There is something in every one of you that waits
and listens for the sound of the genuine in yourself.
It is the only true guide you will ever have.
And if you cannot hear it,
you will all of your life spend your days
on the ends of strings that someone else pulls.

Howard Thurman Whitman

What's right with you is the starting point.
What's wrong with you is beside the point.

Uranda

Whatever you can do, or dream you can, begin it.
Boldness has genius, power, and magic in it.

Johann von Goethe

 WHAT IS STOPPING YOU?

All my life I've always wanted to *be* somebody.
But I see now I should have been more specific.

Jane Wagner

Dream lofty dreams,
and as you dream, so shall you become.
Your vision is the promise of
what you shall one day be.

James Allen

Nothing happens unless first a dream.

Carl Sandburg

115

DOES DYING BEGIN WHEN YOU
STOP DREAMING?

Your imagination is your preview of
life's coming attractions.

Albert Einstein

If you are working on something exciting
that you really care about,
you don't have to be pushed.
The vision pulls you.

Steven Jobs

We distinguish the excellent man from the common man
by saying that the former is the one who
makes great demands on himself,
and the latter,
makes no demands on himself.

José Ortega y Gasset

Everything starts as a daydream.

Larry Niven

I believe in the imagination.
What I cannot see
is infinitely more important
than what I can see.

Duane Michaels

Dream lofty dreams,
so shall you become.
Your vision is the promise of
what you shall at last unveil.

John Ruskin

IF YOU KNEW YOUR CHILD
WOULD TAKE IT,
WHAT ADVICE ABOUT DREAMING
WOULD YOU GIVE?

The opportunities of man are limited
only by his imagination.
But so few have imagination that there are
ten thousand fiddlers to one composer.

Charles F. Kettering

117

If one advances confidently
in the direction of his dreams
and endeavors to live the life which he has imagined,
he will meet with a success unexpected in common hours.
…If you have built castles in the air
your work need not be lost.
That is where they should be.
Now put foundations under them.

Henry David Thoureau

Lord, grant that I may always desire
more than I can accomplish.

Michelangelo

Our plans miscarry because they have no aim.
When a man does not know
what harbor he is making for,
no wind is the right wind.

Seneca

We find no real satisfaction or happiness in life
without obstacles to conquer and goals to achieve.

Dr. Maxwell Maltz

118

It is our duty as men and women to proceed as though the limits of our abilities do not exist.

Pierre Teilhard de Chardin

 IF YOU COULD ACCOMPLISH
JUST ONE GOAL, WHAT WOULD IT BE?

Life always gets harder toward the summit-
the cold increases,
the responsibility increases.

Friedrich Nietzche

The grand essentials
to happiness
in this life are
something to do,
something to love
and something to hope for.

Joseph Addison

Goals are dreams with deadlines.

Diana Scharf Hunt

119

When schemes are laid in advance,
it is surprising how often the circumstances
fit in with them.

William Osler

You will become as small as your controlling desire;
as great as your dominant aspiration.

James Allen

 DO YOU SPEND MORE TIME PLANNING YOUR
TWO-WEEK VACATION OR YOUR LIFE?

Aim at heaven and you will get Earth thrown in.
Aim at Earth and you get neither.

C.S. Lewis

An aspiration is a joy forever,
a possession as real as a landed estate,
a fortune which we can never exhaust
and which gives us year by year a revenue
of pleasurable activity.

Robert Louis Stevenson

To live for some future goal is shallow.
It's the sides of the mountain
that sustain life,
not the top.

Robert M. Pirsig

Establishing goals is all right
if you don't let them deprive you of
interesting detours.

Doug Larson

 DO YOU REMEMBER
TO KEEP YOUR EYE ON THE BALL
AND NOT ON THE SCOREBOARD?

You can have anything you want
if you want it desperately enough.
You must want it with an exuberance
that erupts through the skin
and joins the energy that
created the world.

Sheila Graham

121

The full-grown human being...
is conscious of touching
the highest pinnacle of fulfillment...
when he is consumed in the service of an idea,
in the conquest of the goal pursued.

R. Briffault

There are two things to aim at in life:
first, to get what you want;
and, after that, to enjoy it.
Only the wisest of mankind achieve the second.

Logan Pearsall Smith

 IS IT MORE TRAGIC TO FAIL REACHING
A GOAL OR TO HAVE NO GOAL TO REACH?

When you get in a tight place
and everything goes against you,
till it seems as though you could not
hold on a minute longer, never give up then,
for that is just the place and time that the tide will turn.

Harriet Beecher Stowe

122

EPILOGUE

Before I began creating this book, I believed my function would be that of a somewhat dispassionate researcher, compiling information and adding comments in the form of questions. To my amazement, just the opposite occurred: I became deeply involved on a very personal level. Each thought I read was a reflection of my own doubts, hopes, fears, needs and concerns.

Unlike many other larger collections of thoughts and ideas, the limited scope of this book forced me to ask myself over and over again, "What parts of our human experience are important enough to warrant comments and advice?" In effect, creating this book for you provided me the opportunity to rediscover and recommit myself to values which I am absolutely sure maximize my experience of the joy of living. My wish for you is that some of the thoughts and questions in this book will inspire you to maximize the joy in your life.

Send Us Your Brilliant Thoughts and Provocative Questions!

If you have any BRILLIANT THOUGHTS or PROVOCA-
TIVE QUESTIONS you would like to contribute to sequels in
this series, please send them to us. We would be delighted to
acknowledge your contribution and send you a free copy of the
publication in which it appears. You can mail or e-mail your
thoughts or questions to:

Paul Karasik
Joy of Living Publishing
952 Manhattan Beach Blvd., Ste. 200
Manhattan Beach, CA 90266

E-mail: paul@paulkarasik.com
Website: www.paulkarasik.com

About Paul Karasik

Paul Karasik is an international speaker, author, and peak performance consultant. He is president of The Business Institute, a sales and management consulting company. His list of Fortune 500 clients is a Who's Who of American business. Paul is the author of four books: *Sweet Persuasion*, *Sweet Persuasion for Managers*, *How to Make It Big in the Seminar Business*, and *Seminar Selling*. He is the founder of the American Seminar Leaders Association.

Paul has devoted his life to educating and inspiring individuals in the art and science of living a winning life. He is a multi-talented presenter who combines humor, music, magic, theatrics and audience participation. Paul believes our most priceless resource for achieving success and happiness can be found within us, and has dedicated his life to helping others unleash this unlimited power.

He recently appeared in a national Public Broadcasting System television special, "If My Heart Could Do My Thinking…," based upon his life and work.

Paul lives in Manhattan Beach, California, with his two daughters, Sky and Star.

Looking for More Resources to Grow?

"Success Power" — Music CD

Rock-and-roll your way to success! This compact disc is filled with 12 original, toe-tapping, life-changing songs written by Paul Karasik. Each song has a message about meeting challenges, finding passion and creating satisfying relationships. The musical performances are spectacular with Paul Karasik playing guitar and singing. The musicians who play on this album perform with artists such as Aretha Franklin, Bruce Springsteen and Paul McCartney.

CD/Lyrics included .... $15.00 ($3.00 S/H)

"If My Heart Could Do My Thinking ..." — Video

Discover how to bring more joy, passion and success into your life! By applying Paul Karasik's strategies and principles, you will get connected to your personal Passion Focus Points and unlock the secret to changing your life. Paul uses childhood memories, business lessons and music to convey his message. This program includes several original songs including *Getting Ready* and *Make Your Move* written by Paul.

60 minute Video .... $50.00 ($3.00 S/H)

Business Development Tools

For a complete list and descriptions of business development resources including books, audio tapes and video tapes, please see the Website: www.paulkarasik.com or call 310-545-4994.

Live Presentations by Paul Karasik

If your group or organization is interested in one of Paul's high-energy, multi-media programs, call 310-545-4994 for more information and details

Order Your Personal Growth Resources

_____ **SUCCESS POWER**—Music CD
CD/Lyrics Included .... $15.00 ($3.00 S/H) $_____

_____ **IF MY HEART COULD DO MY THINKING...**
Video .... $50.00 ($3.00 S/H) $_____

_____ **_BRILLIANT THOUGHTS AND_**
PROVOCATIVE QUESTIONS
Book .... $20.00 ($3.00 S/H) $_____

TOTAL | **$** |

PAYMENT METHOD:

❑ **Check:** Payable to The Business Institute (U.S. dollars only)

❑ **Credit Card:** ❑ AmEx ❑ MasterCard ❑ Visa

Credit Card #_____Exp. Date_____

Signature _____

Name _____

Address_____

City _____State/Zip _____

Phone _____Fax _____

Email _____

**For fastest ordering by credit card,
fax this form to 310-545-2346, call 310-545-4994,
or mail this coupon with your check enclosed to:**

**Joy of Living Publishing
952 Manhattan Beach Blvd., Ste. 200
Manhattan Beach, CA 90266**

CPSIA information can be obtained
at www.ICGtesting.com
Printed in the USA
FFHW022349030419
51440910-56884FF